TRIUMPH HOUSE
Poetry with a Purpose

TO LOVE THY NEIGHBOUR...?

Edited by

CHRIS WALTON

First published in Great Britain in 1998 by
TRIUMPH HOUSE
1-2 Wainman Road, Woodston,
Peterborough, PE2 7BU
Telephone (01733) 230749

All Rights Reserved

Copyright Contributors 1998

HB ISBN 1 86161 214 1
SB ISBN 1 86161 219 2

FOREWORD

Over the years poetry has begun to take a place in society and is now one of the most stylish and comfortable ways of expressing true feelings and thoughts.

This anthology is an inspiring and fulfilling collection of poems about the people we encounter most in our everyday lives, *Neighbours*. The poems have been brought together to create a sensational and captivating book of poetry which will inspire both the poetry lover and first time reader.

Nosy, avenging, timid and friendly, neighbours have all been combined to create a close-knit neighbourhood.

The poems vary in length, style and subject making this anthology suitable reading for people of all ages and all walks of life.

Chris Walton
Editor

CONTENTS

Title	Author	Page
Jane	Shirley Lidbetter	1
Neighbours	J Hammond	2
Untitled	Maria Waters	3
Love Thy Neighbour	D Meek	4
Nebula IC133	Sandra Lewis	5
A Total Disaster	Evelyn Balmain	6
Just My Luck	J Wickens	7
The Coward	V J Chapman	8
No Fence	Margaret Andrews	9
Good Neighbours	Steve Newbury	10
The Neighbours	P Williams	11
Old Annie's	Angela Patchett	12
Good Neighbours	Nicholas Winn	13
Our New Neighbours	June Beadnell	14
Good Neighbours	Keith L Powell	15
Infernal Neighbour	Laura Föst	16
My Favourite Neighbours	Chris Key	17
Crossways	Robert D Shooter	18
Neighbours	John Christopher	19
Heaven Or Hell	Dorothy Langdon	20
Tuppence	T B Smith	21
Neighbours	Judith Pryor	22
Cheek By Jowl	Eileen Davis	23
The Widow	Pauline Hamblin	24
Who Are My Neighbours?	Emily Macintosh	25
Night Walker	Rosemary Muncie	26
Neighbours - Here To Stay!	Jeanne Jinks	27
The Gossip	Peggy Howe	28
Mrs Jones	S K Haddad	30
Goody-Ghouls?	Hilary Jill Robson	31
Neighbours From Hell	Margaret M Osoba	32
Neighbourhood Watch	Eileen Handley	33
Those New Neighbours	Reg Morris	34
Our Neighbour	J Facchini	35
Consideration	Elaine McCulloch Smith	36

The Virago	Mary Rutley	37
Noisy Neighbours	Ann Grimwood	38
Pet Hates	Deirdre Rogers	39
Aunty Sue	Jan Lingard	40
'Spaced Out' Neighbours	Freda Baxter	41
Neighbours And Friends	Kerry D Beck	42
It's A Knockout	Kim Montia	43
Neighbours From 'Hell'	William Hayles	44
Unfortunate	K M Clemo	45
Neighbour-Free Zone	Amanda-Lea Manning	46
Goodbye, Saxon Invader	Paul Wadge	48
Good Neighbours?	Marie Dennis	49
Neighbours	B Spencer	50
Neighbours	B Neave	52
My Neighbour	Patricia Weitz	53
Neighbours	O Bushell	54
An Incontinence Of Blood	D V Lockyer	55
Neighbours	Marjory Scott	56
The Good Neighbours' Guide	Emma Jane Soule	57
Food For Africa	J C Lewis	58
No Respect Anymore!	Leigh Smart	59
I Am Blessed	Rowland Patrick Scannell	60
Our Loving Neighbours Of Dunblane	Kenneth E Barker	61
Cefn-Mawr	Doreen King	62
New Neighbours	Alyx Stonehouse	63
To My Neighbour Sue	Rita Hardiman	64
Our Street	Sally Malone	65
Good Neighbours	James Leonard Clough	66
Deceived	Joy Benford	67
Untitled	Julie Boitoult	68
Revenge	Gail Susan Halstead	69
Without A Sound	Rosemary Thomson	70
Neighbours - A Breed Alone	Susan Merrifield	71
Musical Neighbours	Michele Baston	72
Good Neighbour	Anna King	73
Oscar D Kossoloff	E J Butler	74
Little Brenda Brown	Benny H Howell	75

Title	Author	Page
My Neighbours, My Friends	Pauline Uprichard	76
Neighbours	M S Richmond	77
Neighbour From Hell	Colin Allsop	78
From Heaven To Hell Overnight	Barbara Goode	79
The New Neighbours	Jan Ingram McCaffery	80
Look Through My Eyes	Philip Trivett	81
Untitled	Janet Smith	82
The Folk Next Door	Peter Fordham	83
Frankly	Pauline Nash	84
The Neighbours	Hazel Vambria Walters	85
Good Samaritan	Pauline Pullan	86
Blood And Water	David Barrow	87
Neighbours	Chrissi	88
Our Postman	D Sheasby	89
Bless My Neighbour	Michael Darwood	90
Different To Us	Susan Mullinger	91
The State And Me	Dan Pugh	92
Our Neighbours From Heaven	Coleen Bradshaw	93
In The Vast Expanse	Ann G Wallace	94
The Neighbour From Hell!	M Muirhead	96
Neighbours From Mars	David Tallach	98
Number Ten	Sara Russell, Golden Eagles MCC	99
The Neighbour From Hell	Linda Brown	100
Marital Bliss	Yvonne Sewell	101
In-Laws	Carol Dunn	102
On A Hot Dusty Street	Teresita Durkan	103
Life At 80	Veda Dovaston	104
Neighbours	Sylvia Chandler	105
Healthy Living Neighbours	Beatrice Wilson	106

JANE

There's a girl who lives two doors away
You'd never think that we'd get on
I am shy and very quiet
She is loud and full of fun

She's always there to help me out
I never have to ask
When she has my kids to stay the night
It never seems a task

She shouts and hollers at the kids
And they all go back for more
Whether you visit morning noon or night
There's a welcome at her door

It's hard to find a person
Who will always give you time
Whether we sit there doing crosswords
Or just talking we get along fine

If she was ever to move away
I really really would miss her
She isn't just a good friend
To me she is more like a sister.

Shirley Lidbetter

NEIGHBOURS

When someone moves in next to you,
You hope they will be nice,
Because, for the next few years to come,
They could change your life.

When Glenda came to live by me,
I welcomed her with flowers,
She's been a joy for two whole years
Bringing sunshine and no showers.

We laugh a lot - drink cups of tea,
And share a tear or two,
We also share our garden plants
Of red and gold and blue.

We have four cats between us,
And love them all alike,
They live just like their owners,
And never, never fight.

I'm glad that Glenda came to live
In the house next door,
She's young, lively and full of fun,
And has never been a bore.

I'm not so young - but not that old
To enjoy her company,
I'd like to think that she also
Likes living next to me.

J Hammond

UNTITLED

I've talked to friends in Germany, Sweden and Japan
And as I correspond with them
I realise
I still don't know who they are at No 27 or 31
I live at 29
I don't know those beside
I know who lives in Dusseldorf and places world-wide
I still don't talk or see or speak to those around my home
But I take the thought of home when away
So next time I see those at 27 and 31
I'll pass the time of day with them
And remember to ask their names.

Maria Waters

LOVE THY NEIGHBOUR

Our neighbours the people we all love to hate
Is that them banging was that their gate?
A face behind a curtain
No I cannot be certain
Are they in or are they out?
We will soon know if we hear them shout
Bang on the wall let them know you are cross
In this situation who can ever be boss?
I hesitate as I go out of my door
Knowing my luck I'll bump into that bore
I will smile sweetly gritting my teeth
Trying not to show the dislike I feel beneath
Friends say life's too short try to get on
They don't have to listen to music at half past one
So my patience I am endeavouring to keep
I'm sure that's not them talking while I try to sleep
But dear friends do not take it as read
That all neighbours are as bad as I have said
Some next door neighbours are as nice as can be
So why is it they don't live next door to me?

D Meek

NEBULA IC133

Sightless eyes scanned your galaxy,
Found clouds - the fleeting water,
Evaporated seas or tears
Dripped down two million years.

What if you sense our interest,
Fix thoughts on ours
And we meet on night journeys,
Ride our dreams to a half-way house in space.

Match planets -
Show each our suns
And follow the tracks
Where the starlight runs.

Sandra Lewis

A Total Disaster

I've got a new neighbour, a total disaster!
The only noise she doesn't make . . .
She has no ghetto blaster!
It's not just her, her family's worse,
They visit her often here.
Nobody taught them how to close doors,
So they slam them all I fear.
Car doors, house doors, dustbin lids,
My little place shakes with the pressure.
I wonder sometimes that the tiles on the roof
Don't lift up for a total refresher!
They start up the vacuum 9.30 at night
Its humming distracts from my telly,
And her television is on at all hours,
The boom turns my poor knees to jelly.
She has a young kitten, I don't know why,
It persists in flattening my flowers.
It refuses to go in whenever it's called,
And they shout it outside at all hours.
I've had to move my bedroom around
In order to sleep at night.
I wish she'd go back to where she came from . . .
Better still, into space on the next moon shot flight!

Evelyn Balmain

JUST MY LUCK

A man's home is his castle, or so it's said to be,
But no-one reckoned to the neighbours living next to me,
They're noisy and abusive, plain nasty through and through,
And with their colourful language they turn the air bright blue,
If I can't win the Lottery to move to a new address,
I hope they do, so they would move, please wish us all success!

J Wickens

THE COWARD

My neighbours live at No 7
They never speak to me
I moved here just twelve months ago
Yet still they avoid my looks to say 'Hello'
Avert their eyes away

The husband has an awkward walk
Weak-kneed, he looks a wimp
They say he's hen-pecked too
Maybe he's not allowed to say 'Hello'

His wife is blonde, a Yorkshire lass
She must know what he's like
Getting up at 5am
To do malicious damage in the dark

He punctures tyres and scratches cars
Because, in damaging them, he damages those people
He believes have more than him
And this he cannot take

The police arrested him tonight
Thank God, we're so relieved
As we've suspected him so long
And known he was the guilty one
He must not get reprieve

He's caused us so much heartache
Insomnia, anxiety
He's no idea what we've endured
Our sense of well-being undermined
Because of him, a coward.

V J Chapman

NO FENCE

I was never one for friendly chatter,
But I was captivated by Mary my new neighbour,
She often stands by the fence smiling and delivering friendly advice -
'Such a gift to mankind' - so helpful and nice.

Mary always keeps her word if you're in a jam
Truly unique she's genuine - no two-faced sham -
If ever I'm tired and my legs let me down
My shopping will be done by her with a cheerful smile -
No behind-the-door frown.

Cottage pie baking once used to be a problem for me
'Now come on, Della, give me the ingredients
And just watch and see,'
Her expertise has come to my rescue in the kitchen -
Not being a learned and practised cook
Now we spend hours experimenting with many a cookery book.

If I have a problem with my family affairs she's always there
She gives a helping hand if I am due to go to a party
And have nothing to wear
I passed my driving test with her patient help and guidance
Up and down the busy streets, lanes and roads
I had felt guilty imposing - at least her burden,
I have eased her heavy load.

I was never one for friendly chatter
Now my vocabulary is so wide - it's natter, natter, natter,
Mary and I are like two peas in a pod - so in tune
And next month we shall be going on holidays, no fence,
In the sunny summer month of June.

Margaret Andrews

GOOD NEIGHBOURS

Good neighbours, good neighbours,
a blessing! A boon!
Always there when you need them,
they'll be around soon,
with a chat and a cuppa,
o'er fence or o'er wall,
the world put to rights then - no trouble at all!

Good neighbours, good neighbours,
so priceless a gift!
In semi or terrace,
your spirits they'll lift,
praise God that you have them,
for you know they'll be there,
if you've got good neighbours - you haven't a care!

Steve Newbury

The Neighbours

We're tired and listless every day,
Our nerves are shattered as well,
And this could go on till the middle of May,
'Cause we've got 'the neighbours from Hell'.

Since February the noise at night,
Hasn't stopped for a single second,
It's no good asking for them to stop,
I'm afraid they just wouldn't listen.

Usually they cause no bother,
In fact, you'd hardly know they were there,
But when spring comes, they go quite mad,
Which drives us to despair.

It started when we built the pond,
For goldfish, carp and such,
And then the toads and frogs moved in,
We should have known as much.

From Feb till May they mate with relish,
Croaking and calling in glee,
Water thrashing, they leap and cavort,
Searching for a female who's free.

The fish have retreated to the bottom,
The toads' tastes are just not fussy,
If they can't find a female to charm and cajole,
A fish will do quite nicely.

By the beginning of May there's peace at last,
We can go to bed with no fear,
The jungle nights and noisy neighbours,
Are gone for another year.

P Williams

OLD ANNIE'S

You moved in,
I saw you arrive
tall, slim and bearded
I fancied you like mad.
You were aware of me
but it took friends
to suggest
dinner for four
so we could meet.
That was the beginning
of a friendship,
support and fun.
We lived so close
we saw each other
at our worst
and best -
there was no pretence.
But when love
knocked on our doors
up came the fears,
past hurt
not resolved,
locked each of us in -
our own houses.
The sadness and anger,
longing and hurt
was made worse
by our closeness
because neither
could let the other in.

Angela Patchett

GOOD NEIGHBOURS

Good neighbours cast a friendly eye
  On gardens, lawns and lanes
Will stop to chat and ask about
  Your house and aches and pains;
They'll go on errands if you're ill
  Whatever time of day
And keep a lookout on your house
  Whenever you're away;
No worries when the milkman comes
  Or postmen leave the mail,
Good neighbours take your things inside
  With grace and without fail
They'll mend a broken mower, and
  Know where the fuses are,
If broken down they'll give a hand
  And tinker with the car
A baby-sitter? They'll oblige
  Your pleasure is their wish
They'll worm the dog and groom the cat
  Find time to feed the fish;
Good neighbours care and never swear
  Are honest and polite,
The main thing is they're always there
  Come day or dead of night.

Nicholas Winn

OUR NEW NEIGHBOURS

They came to view and poke about,
They even had a dig at grout!
He stood and looked aghast, while *she*
Went to view it from a tree!

They both decided it would do,
Then had to deter quite a few;
Many sought to view the property,
They guarded it with great dexterity!

They both were into DIY -
Had their sights set really high.
They worked with purpose and with flair,
Their cries of merriment filled the air!

Soon a cosy home they'd made,
All their plans were deftly laid;
They soon were parents of renown,
Their home was just the best in town!

Soon some young ones we did see,
Played about and tchacked with glee;
Then we looked up to see the cause,
Our new neighbours - black Jackdaws!

June Beadnell

GOOD NEIGHBOURS

Hey they are good neighbours
Never make a sound
We just never see them
We think that they have gone to ground.

Hey they are good neighbours
We never see a car
Somehow they come and go
But we never know where they are.

Hey they are good neighbours
Do they ever get any mail?
As far as we know
It could be up for sale.

Keith L Powell

INFERNAL NEIGHBOUR

Various neighbours I have had
All have been good, but one was bad.

It took place in England years ago
When that neighbour from Hell became my foe.
It was all because of a house I'd bought,
And his own plan to buy it came to nought.
Just like mine, his chance was there,
However, I beat him fair and square.
He never forgave me from that day,
And about me spiteful things he'd say.
Then some iron he threw on my drive one night,
Hoping I'd not see it where there was no light.
So I'd p'raps ruin my car or have a crash,
For I only just missed getting a bash.
He'd stand at his corner some days near the road,
Sticking his stomach out like a fat old toad,
So oncoming traffic I could not see
Which might possibly cause a collision for me.
Those were *but two* of malicious things he did,
Just because on a house I'd him outbid.
Soon, I sold it to strangers and then moved on,
And wasn't I glad because I had gone
Away from that bad neighbour at last
To live near good neighbours - *oh!* Such a contrast.

Laura Föst

MY FAVOURITE NEIGHBOURS

For some eighty years, life's had high spots and low
But now age and disability, beginning to show,
One depends on her man, for care day and night
Though he's eighty eight, he tries to keep bright
But frustration causes friction, and some days are tough
Care in the community isn't always enough;
The other dear lady lives on her own
Her link to friends and family, the telephone
Struggling to cope each and every day
To stay in her home and not go away;
The help available has to fit in, with many more
So timing is difficult and never know for sure
Who or when it will be, this can make one feel
Like a second-class citizen, it's not a fair deal;
Doctors and nurses are frustrated too,
When both need reassurance, there's little they can do,
All these two ladies need, is tender loving care
Just to know, that someone is there,
A kind word or deed makes the day so much brighter,
The heart fill with hope and the load a little lighter;
These are just two that I see, but there's many more
Who would welcome a friendly visitor, on opening the door,
So don't think that someone else will go round,
Be neighbourly, pop in, make sure they're safe and sound.

Chris Key

CROSSWAYS

Barley car-park, location for quiet peaceful walk.
Found car-park full to overflowing! Awed
by all the traffic but park on the road - a fork
yielding a space. Lots of folk milling about - toyed
with idea of abandoning the walk - killing
it! But with spectators greeting winning runners -
six mile up Pendle Hill and Boar's Clough -passing
quickest straight away but as I walk the others -
some seemed fit and happy; others give impression
would rather take up basket-work or cut their nails!
Some of their terrified masks connected with some
agonies of shared journey - not just today's - hails
joy and bitterness, forgiveness and death, on cross,
spirit and breath, word redeeming us our deep loss.

Robert D Shooter

NEIGHBOURS

Our neighbours do affect us all
for no one lives alone.
Perhaps it is that garden hedge
that's got so overgrown.

Perhaps it is that broken fence
they're promising to mend,
but promises so often made
are broken in the end.

Perhaps it is that teenage son
that parties such a lot,
and when you've asked about the noise
abuse is all you've got!

Perhaps you think of all the times
you've done a kindly deed,
yet they have never once helped out
when you have been in need.

The neighbours, either side of me
are really 'chalk' and 'cheese'.
One side they are a dream come true
and always keen to please.

The other side? Perhaps it's best
my lips stay tightly sealed.
A trouble never caused at all
is like a trouble healed.

Just make the best of everything
and life may soon improve.
If not, then someone's telling you
it could be time to move!

John Christopher

HEAVEN OR HELL

They say that you are neighbours from hell,
But from what I have seen how can I tell,
From the fleeting glance I had,
I am not sure if good or bad,
You drove past in your posh car with your noses in the air,
Knowing I was your neighbour you didn't even care,
Who are you! With your superior ways,
You came into the world, you live your days
The same as I, you'll also die!
But no you have decided I am not worth knowing,
Well that's your loss not mine,
That way you don't have to be nasty or kind,
And yes! That suits me also I don't really mind,
I lived my life before you came,
Having you for a neighbour is no gain.

Dorothy Langdon

TUPPENCE

My puppy was friendly with those neighbours
Who looked after her while I was at work.
It was a friendly cul-de-sac for people
Whose ages ranged from babyhood to retirement.

We dropped in on each other for a natter
On how our houses were run,
Our gardens looked and if our cars were clean,
Forming a relationship with each other.

In just over a year I passed the exams,
Adding qualifications to my name,
When an accident in my car
Landed me in hospital for months - disabled.

But my puppy was well protected.
Neighbours 'baby-sat' my little dog
Until my parents arrived
To be met by caring neighbours.

After that I moved away
Where my dog could wander at will,
Finding food from a willing hand
And loving to guard my lawn.

My dog has, sadly, passed away
But this cul-de-sac isn't so young
Or friendly as it should be
To live together happily.

T B Smith

NEIGHBOURS

Everywhere we live, urban or rural,
We cannot escape neighbour from hell;
On TV they give us all a good laugh,
But if next door you just have to sell.

There's one rule for them and another for others,
With only thought for their own needs;
The world exists for them to enjoy,
No laws or thought for their misdeeds.

They argue over an inch of land,
Marking their territory like a wild beast,
They think the worst of everyone else,
On paranoia and hatred they feast.

There's a natural law in the human race,
Respect and fear taught by mothers;
We've all used our power over someone weaker,
And yielded under the strength of others.

But with these neighbours who are bullies,
They have never experienced fears,
They charge through life doing what they want,
Caring nothing for anyone's tears.

The law is not interested, it's far too soft,
For people who thrive on power;
The *hair of the dog* is the only thing,
That will make these animals cower.

So move in neighbours who are stronger than them,
Let them see what it's like to receive abuse;
And when they demand help from the law, which they will,
Tell them to *stew in their own juice*.

Judith Pryor

CHEEK BY JOWL

Four short years
Cheek by jowl
Familiar strangers
Exchanging pleasantries
At points of connection
In our separate lives.

Your lives have a rhythm
I dread and envy
A routine and order
That rivals the chaos
Beneath my roof
Behind my door.

Telling glimpses
Complete a picture
Laundry on Monday
Fish and chips on Friday
Terry Wogan every morning
A week in Ireland each spring.

A For Sale board outside my door
Now we relinquish our brief encounter
Yours was a still point in my turning world
Your lives cheerfully bound by ritual
Predictable as the seasons
Ballast against the passage of time.

Eileen Davis

THE WIDOW

The ceremonies are over, respects given and the mourners all gone.
You are left to wrap the comfort of the house,
around you now all on your own.
It is only during this time, that finality, really starts the reality going.
Tears will keep flowing in fits and starts, as memories tumble
between your brain and your heart.
All this is normal, a very necessary, healing procedure,
just remember, you have a neighbour nearby to call,
if you need her.

Pauline Hamblin

WHO ARE MY NEIGHBOURS?

Neighbours makes you think of,
The people next door,
The grumps across the street,
And the mice under the floor.
But no,
These neighbours are very strange,
Far out of viewing range.
Not in your country,
Continent or planet.
In fact,
They're out of this world.
Tucked up and curled,
Far far away.
A visit would take you
More than a day!

Emily Macintosh (10)

NIGHT WALKER

Bricks are hard
Like words at the side of the house
Climbing where chimneys
Mine and next door display
The littered tablecloth
From which we like to measure near and far
Or watch the floral moon take out a star
Whatever. This arrangement going on
Unmindful of our quarrel.

The chimneys are friends
Companions in mutual agreement
And twin walls from below
Seem to lean together
Narrowing the gap, the gap, the gap.
Their kitchen window spills some light
Sticks of orange march the garden trees
Into a wayward sorting for the night.

Unwanted voices
Do they suspect I am out here
Watching our friendly chimneys?

Rosemary Muncie

NEIGHBOURS - HERE TO STAY!

Next door there is an old churchyard.
Fractured, mossy-veiled stones lean here
Half hidden in grass, ivy trailed.
These long dead have no marble urns,
Their house names are gaudy lichens
No lawns - just brambles and tall ferns.

A prowling cat probes the lush growth,
Sharpening claws on arthritic trees,
Ready to stalk, pounce, play and seize
Some small, unwary trespasser.

Fallen stones are stacked to allow
Mechanised mower and wedding groups.
Guests pose under the ancient boughs
And fret when dark clouds make shadow.
Paper petals litter the ground.
The bells are dumb. Folks long gone.
Night reveals the belfry lamp aglow
While out of the night comes the sound
Of an owl hooting to the moon.
Leaves shroud fading epitaphs.

Some weathered stones reveal those names
Once well known in village life.
We mourn their long lost skills and blame
Prior generations for their greed,
And our addiction to mindless speed.
Next door is my retreat from *now*.

Jeanne Jinks

THE GOSSIP

My neighbour is a gossip,
She's not so very young.
When I'm feeling naughty,
I call her Mrs Tongue.

I try hard not to see her,
I'll go to any length.
But when she's got me cornered,
She rattles on in strength.

Have you heard the news dear?
They say it's going to rain.
The ambulance came for Mollie,
They say she's rolled in pain.

Tommy whatsit's out again,
That's not his name you know.
They say he robbed a bank,
But that's a while ago.

They're keeping chickens over there,
Cor, they don't half stink.
They haven't got a bath you know,
They wash down in the sink.

Young Susie's in the family way,
They say she's having twins.
Old Fred the post was in the pub,
He's wobbly on his pins.

Do you remember Martha?
The one that married Sid.
They had to take her off again,
They say she's flipped her lid.

Goodness me, look at the time,
You ain't half kept me talking,
Got to get the dinner on,
And take the dog a walking.

I'd like to know who *they* are,
They have a lot to answer for.
I suppose I must be grateful,
That *they* do not live next door.

Peggy Howe

MRS JONES

She lived alone in a house of stone,
My neighbour for countless years;
Widow forlorn, no one to own
Yet sheltered away her tears.
The day was hot and I did not
Consider to light my fire,
But I did spot her chimney pot
With smoke rising up higher.
I rang her bell, my pulse did swell,
I worried she caught a chill
But I could tell that all was well:
She seemed too bright to be ill.
She looked and turned, the coal fire burned,
The hearth was covered with dust;
The hot air churned, summer returned
To discomfit the robust.
I asked her why the flame was high
On a day, warm as could be;
She was not shy of her reply:
It is company for me.

S K Haddad

GOODY-GHOULS?

Neighbours from heaven? Neighbours from hell?
Ours are neither, together we gel,
Not in and out homes to borrow or scrounge,
Our lives too busy to natter or lounge,
Look after each other also chattels,
There is not a soul who tittle tattles,
Take in parcels or registered post,
Maybe a party; a neighbour plays host,
Exchange our skills, sometimes a plant,
Feed the pets, give seedlings to transplant,
Loan them our mini when their car breaks down,
Or join up for dinner somewhere in town,
Watch over houses when they're away,
Keep it secret, times they holiday,
We know they're there if help is required,
Ready and willing when aid is desired,
Should ever they think of making a move,
Without a doubt we'd disapprove.
Neighbours all around, north, south, east and west,
We live in paradise; they are the best,
No argument! Where we all dwell
We've angels from heaven, not neighbours from hell,
There's only one snag that worries me,
Too good to live? Except the cemetery!

Hilary Jill Robson

NEIGHBOURS FROM HELL

Purdy thought he'd like a gas fire
Of the latest, up to date.
So he ups and whacks the fireplace
Into bits, knocks out the grate.
        Bangs and smashes,
        Whams and bashes,
Crack! The back fire-boiler's burst.
Then the water scoots and rushes
Through the house while Purdy cursed.

But undaunted, some time later
On the clown decides to go,
Saws right through a leaky gas pipe.
'Whoosh!' - the building's all aglow.
With a 'boom' it's blown to pieces,
Fragments flying through the air.
Gone the old familiar faces,
All to glory - none to spare,
And the neighbours all in heaven
Angels are, like little Nell.
Purdy's wife had fought the devil -
Now *she* rules the roost in hell!

Margaret M Osoba

NEIGHBOURHOOD WATCH

'Would you like to join in a Neighbourhood Watch?'
said the lady who stood at the door,
Yes, I thought it a good idea,
but somebody had thought of it before,
She does it single handed,
from seven right through to ten,
So rarely does she leave her post,
if so she's soon back again.

She doesn't seem to miss a thing,
she knows our every move,
And then if she's caught peeping,
dodges out of sight so smooth,
She watches you get the milk,
and empty your mail box,
She likes to see what you've got on,
she's such a sly old fox.

But I would bet you ten to one,
that if a burglar came,
She'd be so busy watching him,
she'd treat him just the same,
She'd forget what game he was up to,
she'd be eyeing him up as a man,
It would probably only register,
when he put your goods in a van.

Eileen Handley

THOSE NEW NEIGHBOURS

We dread to see the van next door, will they be neighbours from hell?
Looking for the signs, umpteen children, and dogs uncontrolled,
only time will tell.
Days go by, we're losing weight, there are no signs that tell it all.
We haven't seen a soul, for the cup of sugar, not a call.
Suspicion grows, it's too good to be true, have they committed suicide,
Or perhaps they visualise that we're unsociable and so proceed
to hide.
It's easy to let imagination run away with us, and tend to get those
thoughts all wrong,
We've listened to accounts of noisy neighbours, where objection's
really strong.
Sitting down contemplating moving to somehow avoid conflict,
A knock comes on the door 'visitors are not welcome', a bad time
they have picked.
An attractive lady says 'Sorry, I've not called before, we didn't
want to fuss,
You see we're rather shy newly-weds and it's all new to us.
We've moved in next door, it's our first house, we want to do
things right.
We don't want to be a nuisance, but we were fixing pictures rather
late last night.'
There's embarrassment, cups of tea, and invitations to put our
minds at rest.
We could have ideal neighbours,
It seems we're the ones who should be put to the test.

Reg Morris

OUR NEIGHBOUR

Though grief was deep he didn't moan
When he was sadly left alone
Surviving now his much-loved wife
He trod a lonely path through life.
A quiet man he went his way
Silently mourning every day.
With endless jobs he filled his hours
How he loved his vegetables and flowers.
The garden, always his delight
Filled every day and summer night.

So many knew the benefit of his generosity,
Plants, cuttings, flowers and produce, given abundantly.
How freely too he gave away that knowledge kept in store
Much can be learned from gardening books, but he knew
                                                                        so much more.

These months the plot has seen neglect, the grass is never mown,
His greenhouse gone, the space that's left with nettles overgrown
Well used tools have been laid down, his spade left by the shed
As rampantly the weeds spring up, in border, frame and bed.
We look back in admiration at the way he carried on
Because the house is empty now, our friend next door is gone
We'll welcome our new neighbours, they're all part of life's plan
As it goes on I'm sure we won't forget that dear old man.

J Facchini

CONSIDERATION

Consideration
is a way of life.
Consideration
avoids strife.

Quietly tread
along the way,
to courtesy wed
by night and day.

Upon your neighbour's space
do not encroach,
filling your ways
with reproach.

Your neighbour's need
you do not know.
By selfish deed
you cause woe.

Consideration
means the art
of self-denying comprehension
of another's part.

In this post Christian age
the few considerate live in stress,
exhausted in the carnage
of this humanist mess.

Elaine McCulloch Smith

THE VIRAGO

He looked like a Sumo wrestler
She - as tiny as they come
He was quiet and unassuming
And firmly underneath her thumb.

Pamela shrieked from morn till evening
And her daughters joined in too
Billingsgate had come to Stoneleigh -
That became the general view.

When she argued with her husband
She went on and on and on!
My guests asked me how he endured it
Since they could not - and soon were gone.

How could such a tiny creature
Shout with a force to wake the dead?
How cold a man the size of Dudley
Endure the horrid things she said?

Oh! For peace in house and garden
That became my constant prayer
Oh! The peace when Pam departed
God help neighbours - everywhere!

Mary Rutley

Noisy Neighbours

Each morning they wake me, with their constant noise,
Playing with the control like it's some kind of toy
No consideration for the people who live above
I can't take it anymore, I've just had enough
I'd give them a piece of my mind
But it's not in my nature to be so unkind
It's not that I disapprove of them having fun,
But their music always starts at half past one.
One day though I'll even the score, put my speakers
                                        outside their front door
I'll ring their doorbell at 3am
I wonder who, will be complaining then.

Ann Grimwood

PET HATES

I am a little Scottie dog,
Dougal is my name.
I have a pleasant garden
In which to have a game.

Whether I am playing
Or basking in the sun,
I love my little garden
Where I can have a run.

There's just one thing that spoils it -
My dreadful neighbours three.
They taunt me and torment me
And watch me from a tree.

They trespass in my garden
And leave an awful smell,
And, if I didn't hide it,
They'd steal my bone as well.

I bark at them and chase them,
I growl and snarl and bite,
But always I just miss them
When they take their flight.

Oh, how I hate my neighbours,
They bug me more than gnats.
You'll see why when I tell you
My neighbours are - three cats!

Deirdre Rogers

AUNTY SUE
(With thanks for all the help, and the friendship given)

My mummy says, when I was born
You paced the room from dusk 'til dawn.
When Daddy had to work away
You helped Mum almost every day;
And when she felt both sad and blue
My mummy always turned to you.
You baby-sit when Dad is home
So Mum and Dad can be alone.
You walk me, each week, into town
And push my buggy up and down.
You buy me sweets for after tea,
You're good at looking after me.
You don't mind playing games, or noise,
Or stepping over books and toys.
Mum goes to work so you help out,
I know one thing without a doubt
If you didn't help she'd be hard pressed,
My mummy says you are the best.
You're Mummy's friend, but you've become
My Aunty Sue - my second mum.

Jan Lingard

'SPACED OUT' NEIGHBOURS

The truth is out there. Are they here?
Aliens probing our atmosphere?
Little green men who come from Mars
Beyond the outer limits of the stars
Flying to earth through space and time
Communicating with a sign?

Others from where? No way to tell
A mysterious crash-landing at Roswell
To know the whole truth would amaze
Long arms, big heads, almond eyes - The Greys
Questions to Area 51 in vain
Security under tightened rein

Then there are the zombie kind
Who invade your body and your mind
And circulate amongst your neighbours
Doing them more harm than favours
Those piercing screams shock you to the core
It's him again - the chap next door

Yet never complain or he just might
Zap you with a beam of light!

Freda Baxter

NEIGHBOURS AND FRIENDS

We help our neighbours in times of stress,
We help our neighbours to a new address.
We help our neighbours in many a way,
We help our neighbours be it night or day.

There are no limits nor out of bounds,
It's the unspoken love that is profound.
We'll care today and we'll care tomorrow,
We'll share your joy and we'll share your sorrow.

If in trouble large or trouble small,
You know we're here so give us a call.
With us beside you the problem we'll share,
No thanks needed for you know we care.

Some people think that life's black or white,
But they're really mistaken for that's not right.
Much of life is spent in shades of grey,
Where friendships are formed in unbreakable clay.

We smile and laugh and cry together,
We share the sun and stormy weather.
We have our life and you have yours,
But it's all interwoven like a maze of doors.

We see your car draw up at the gate,
Caring not if it's early or whether it's late.
Your life may be whole or torn in tatters,
But you are here and that's all that matters.

Kerry D Beck

It's A Knockout

Playing 'It's A Knockout'
Economics is the test
Monetary union
Where each team does their best

But squabbles break out at the start
When purse strings are the aim
To push aside opponents
Are the tactics of the game

Round two now and Eurodollars
Must be rolled along
The market's breadth by each team
And the French are looking strong

They've played their Joker early
And the Germans lag behind
The British haven't joined in yet
Their entry form not signed

Round three sets the interest rates
How high can they be stacked?
Each European member
Confident they have it cracked

But, oh dear, none can beat the clock
Their time has run right out
And all across the Union
The people scream and shout

Kim Montia

Neighbours From 'Hell'

My heart is almost breaking
As my tale of woe I now tell
I must voice the steps I'm taking
Regarding my neighbours from 'Hell'!

When you ask Christ, 'Who is my neighbour?'
He will always quote the man by the road,
And the Samaritan rewarded for his labour,
Saved by the good which he sowed.

So I pray for the person who slights me,
I love all who don't love me back,
I forgive all injustice I see,
I show the way to God, which we lack.

But to get back to my reason for speaking,
My views on my neighbours I'll tell,
I love them and their salvation I'm seeking,
You see, I'm saving my neighbours from 'Hell'!

William Hayles

Unfortunate

Have I been used and abused
Discarded in the gutter
As a whimsical flutter?
I hear not even your mouth utter a mutter
A stammer or stutter,

Here in the gutter I rest
Garbage on my vest mud upon my breast,
Left out with the rubbish rotting and foul
Not a friend or pal,
How can this be so?

Show some kindness to the pauper, the peasant
The stench so unpleasant,
The lowest of the low,
Please

Call yourself a Christian?
Call yourself civilised?
You're the ones I despise
All front and no thought,
An unfortunate waif.

K M Clemo

NEIGHBOUR-FREE ZONE

Somewhere deep in Hampshire's countryside,
Nestling alongside woods of oak and pine
Sits a white cottage quite perfectly;
Stone walls keep the rooms cool in high summer,
And during the winter nights the warmth of the open fires,
Is trapped within their protective layers.
A neighbourless domain, no troubles or cross words exchanged.
No noise or pollution to destroy this paradise.
I treasure my solitude and am at one with nature.
I often sit and watch the stars twinkle in the navy skies of night,
The silence seldom broken, perhaps the rustle of leaves may intervene,
Or a deer gently walking with her fawn, sniffing the air as
                                            she strolls on.
If I wake before the clock strikes seven, I may see her from my
                                            kitchen window,
The dawn is always beautiful, when the rain is far away;
A fine mist often hovers a foot from the ground,
Creating a sense of mystery, drifting without sound.
The rabbits rise early, glossy coats shining in the early morning
                                            sunshine,
Noses twitching, as they nibble at grass and my plants,
                                            which can be vexing.
The dawn chorus is amazing, by four o'clock it is in full swing,
Deafening to the newly woken ear,
But soon the chirping sounds blend into the background.
Late summer evenings are always best, I sit on my porch and
                                            watch the sun go down.
Hearing nature settling down for the night,
Sometimes a friendly toad hops in to say *goodnight,*
Whilst my cats are intrigued by this strange visitor, I hastily
                                            remove the temptation,
Leaving them quite miffed.

The red and golden skies soon sink beneath the skyline,
The warmth of the day still lingering in the air;
Leaving me wondering at my fortunate situation,
A haven, somewhere in Hampshire's lovely countryside.

Amanda-Lea Manning

GOODBYE, SAXON INVADER

This ancient country that was ours,
soon laid to waste by soulless Saxons,
will gently slumber 'til one day,
in all her glory she'll awake.

Saxon invader, hear this now,
you'll never break this will of ours,
day by day you'll think we're beaten,
'til the time when we'll awaken.

Many times you've tried to beat us,
even tried to kill our language,
but even though you glance straight past us,
never once your grip is loosened.

Now the day of freedom's near,
when we in Wales will choose our future,
not for us the Saxon ruler,
but at last, self-rule is near.

Those who wish the Saxon ruler,
make your home across the water,
we in Wales deserve much better,
Wales is where the Welsh must rule.

Paul Wadge

GOOD NEIGHBOURS?

You lived beside me every day
We watched the children laugh and play
You knew the Lord and kept His way
        But yet you never told me.

For years I felt an ache inside
I kept it from you, tried to hide
You had the answer to my pride
        But yet you never told me.

The years rolled by and slipped away
We still shared moments of the day
I had such doubts I could not say
        But yet you never told me.

Then came the day you shared your Lord
The light poured in with every word
Assurance came, the truth was heard
        Praise God at last you told me.

Marie Dennis

NEIGHBOURS

When they moved in next door to us
we thought it would be fun.
The house was empty for so long,
how could we have been so wrong?

Well, they were three and so were we,
they had a girl, and us a boy
good playmates, or so we thought,
when she was three and ours was four.

Now Annie was so cute,
a little blonde haired mite
but right from the start she wasn't allowed
to play with our red headed Mike.

They explained it thus
their treasure and their pride
could not be allowed to play with boys,
who could be - well - a little rough.
She was being brought up a lady you see,
and this did not include
playing with a he.

So, while Annie screamed and sulked
our Mike had lots of fun.
In splash pool, sand-pit, beloved bike,
and shared it all with friends of like.

But when they moved, oh joy, oh bliss
our snobby neighbours gone,
We did not miss them, no, not at all,
no need now to build a wall!

Now our new neighbours are just great,
we blend nicely, thank you mate.
No screams or shouts to disturb the peace
in fact you could say,
all hostilities have now have ceased.

B Spencer

NEIGHBOURS
(In celebration of the Stormont Castle Agreement signed 10.4.98)

Men of violence
You've had your day,
Go, greet your neighbours
Watch the young children go out and play.

Give them an inheritance
They can enjoy,
No longer looking over their shoulders
For the hammer or boulders
For the men of strife
For the bullet or the knife.

Walk side by side
Cross over the fences
Speak words to each other
Acknowledge your sister and brother.

When the woman
Stands by her gate
Exchange friendly words
To herald this new day.

Oh, glorious time
When peace will be sublime
The streets will be calm
The sun will blaze forth
To proclaim for all who want to hear,

Men of violence
You've had your day,
Watch the young children go out and play.
Speak to each other
And hear what each has to say.

B Neave

MY NEIGHBOUR

She was an old lady of ninety-four
Camellias and clematis clung round her front door
Only once I glimpsed her dressed all in grey
On the tiny path bordered by box and by bay
Dragging her dust-bag down to the gate
With a burden, invisible, increasing the weight,
She stole me a glance, weary and worn,
As pulling and puffing she trudged along.

Silently reaching the desired destination
I sought to engage her in conversation:
Her life was part of a period long gone
An only brother lost his life on the Somme,
Now deaf, dejected, contemporaries dead,
Her sole pleasure was her garden she said
Ceasing to feel of this world a part
In nature she seemed nearer God's heart.

Came the dawn my neighbour had joined her friends
In the world hereafter that never ends,
As her spirit winged its way to the kingdom on high
Never a soul was there, there to cry -
Yet her companions, the birds, broke into song
As though they had knowledge of what lay beyond:
But small house and garden wore an air forlorn
Their little old lady they appeared to mourn,
Giant sunflowers, untended, hung huge black heads
Trees dripped tears on silent summer beds
The wind, it sighed and moaned around the cobbled yard
Alternately blowing soft and quite hard
Tossing the bin lid in regular motion
Creating sounds of a toll bell recording devotion.

Patricia Weitz

NEIGHBOURS

My neighbour is
A sweet, old lady
To look at
But . . .

When she's angry
We all hide
Inside.
In the house
In the garden
Behind a bush.

She doesn't like
Boys you see
And I have two
Sons
Living with me.

She's got a thing
About boys.
She doesn't like
Them playing
Football.
She doesn't like
Them playing
Cricket.
She won't give
Them their
Ball back.

My neighbour is
A sweet old lady
To look at
But . . .

O Bushell

AN INCONTINENCE OF BLOOD

There's a man in the flat upstairs dying without reprieve
The medics can interfere only,
Containing the pain sometimes but not the slow, seeping
                                       flood of inevitability.
He makes little fuss and never seems to rant
Against his life of wet sheets which he cleans himself each morning
Of a blood incontinence.
How does he greet each day?
Grateful on waking to new despair?
Does he fear to wake and to fall asleep?

My father is his neighbour downstairs,
Who keeps the to and fro of Samaritan and friend.
Makes him cups of tea, listens and replies.
But Dad is also reliving my mother's death.
He stays as long as he can cope then hurries downstairs to be upset,
To do the raging and the blaming for them both.

D V Lockyer

NEIGHBOURS

Where can I possibly sleep tonight -
In the bedroom or in the lounge?
It'll make little different whichever I choose
For there's noise in both different times of the night
From neighbours with lifestyles as different from mine
As they seem from one another;
Whose one thing in common is devil-may-care
About who lives beside them and how they might fare.

Two youngsters are renting adjacent to me
And another is renting below
Who play loud music and bang their doors
Very often at weekends 'til 3am
When the middle-aged milkman below-but-one
Goes off to work with a roar of his car
While his wife 'gets cracking' the rest of the night
Crashing at intervals through until light.

It wasn't like that when I bought my flat
Some fifteen years ago;
Then *I* was one of the youngest lessees
And my elderly neighbours were bourgeoisie
But later died, and those who bought
Were caught in the negative equity trap
And rented out when they could not sell
Oh! Absentee landlords, you're making life hell!

Marjory Scott

THE GOOD NEIGHBOURS' GUIDE

For me a good neighbour should be
Someone you can always turn to
When you're out of sugar, or need a hand
Your neighbour should be there for you.

If you're out and it rains on your washing
A good neighbour would take it in,
If you're having a very loud party
They shouldn't complain about the din.

When you just want a coffee and a chat
Your neighbour's door should always be open.
They're somebody you can borrow things from
When yours have all been broken.

They should tell you all the gossip
As it's nice to know what's going on,
But when you confide in a neighbour
It should be a secret all life long.

So if you're looking for a new house
Use this as a good neighbours' guide
Keep it with you, and please use it -
Don't be taken for a ride.

Now I'm sure you've seen the programme
It's called 'The Neighbours From Hell'.
Well mine could've even starred in it,
But what do you look for - how can you tell?

I suppose they have to live somewhere,
But why next door to me?
I'd be happier if they lived on an island
With nothing for miles - except the sea.

Emma Jane Soule

FOOD FOR AFRICA

Oh Lord,
There is a country,
Who are my neighbours.
Where food is scarce,
And water is dry.
Its people are dying now,
It needs my help,
So through you,
I ask you now,
Please give them food,
Please give them water,
But most of all,
Please give them life.

J C Lewis

NO RESPECT ANYMORE!

Broken windows - glass everywhere, they've smashed my fence again
My neighbours are living hell - a menace - a real pain
My brand new car has been scratched by someone with a key
Why don't they leave me well alone, why do they pick on me

Mouthfuls of abuse when you confront these young boys
You can play out in the street but don't bring out your toys
Playing football in the street or up against the wall
The police don't want to know so who am I supposed to call?

Living in the garden - maybe all summer long
The smell of barbies and parties - do two rights make a wrong?
No respect for their elders - no respect for anything
They're the neighbours from hell - trouble's all they bring.

Neighbours who will not help you, even in an emergency
Next time it might be them - then no favour's due
Children left to roam all day of their own free will
Never once checked upon, until they come home with the Old Bill.

Neighbours from hell, no respect, never stopping to consider
Anybody but themselves as through life they slither
Put your house up for sale and if you're lucky enough to sell
Vet each buyer carefully and only sell to the next
                                         neighbours from hell.

Leigh Smart

I Am Blessed

Can it be that the heavens have blessed me
I have good neighbours that I called friends
I know without a spoken word they will help
If ever a need and in their quiet way look after me
What more can I ask - I have the beauty of the earth
And I have good neighbours to share my days.
Amen.

Rowland Patrick Scannell

OUR LOVING NEIGHBOURS OF DUNBLANE

That moment of terror that once hit *Dunblane*
And the context of which - must not happen again.
For those holding grief ask 'Oh why, tell us why
did the Lord allow this - from His kingdom on high?'

'There is no real answer' a priest will explain.
'In this cruel world evil strikes with such pain.'
The teacher, young children, so dear to one's heart,
Are now with the Lord - with their loved ones apart.

All those who have suffered such grief in their loss,
Had to pay for man's sin - like our Lord on the Cross.
One cannot console those dear souls left behind;
But *our* love and prayer still brings peace to sad mind.

Although our Lord could not halt sudden harm;
He was there at 'the Gate' with such love - outstretched arm.
'Suffer all little children to come unto Me,
Where My Kingdom awaits - and Great Love is for Thee'.

For those dear ones departed - so young in this life,
Are now free from all evil, in our world full of strife.
Although their dear presence will always be there,
They are now with our Lord - and His Peace, loving care.

Kenneth E Barker

CEFN-MAWR

He whispered gently not to go
To the small place called Cefn-Mawr.
Here in Clwyd, this strange village stands,
Enticing in its fertile lands,
But Flexsys factory's raging crown
Spills out and out its churning smoke,
The mists of fright creep slowly down,
And people huddle in their homes.
So when you spot the raging tower,
Don't dare to think of stopping here.
Just put your foot down in your car,
And drive on past the whiffing vapour.

Doreen King

NEW NEIGHBOURS

We've lived here for nearly two years,
After we put aside all of our fears.

Will we be too noisy, for the old couple next door?
Will my children bug them? But what are children for?

Will our choice of curtains clash with theirs?
Will we both annoy them? Both of us swears.

Will our choice of garden plants be to their taste?
They're not as colourful or as well spaced.

They'll hear all our rowing through the walls,
When we do the washing, they'll view our smalls.

Our worries were unnecessary it turns out
We had absolutely nothing to fret about.

They've turned out much better than the neighbours we had,
But really I have to say that, they're my mum and dad.

Alyx Stonehouse

TO MY NEIGHBOUR SUE

As I am disabled,
I need help every day
With small things and big things,
To live a normal way.

The phone is always handy
Should I be in trouble,
You hear my voice, fly through the hedge,
And land here at the double.

When I needed nursing,
Some jobs weren't very nice,
But you never blinked an eyelid,
You didn't think twice.

What with shopping and cooking
And picking things up too,
Then washing hair and bedclothes,
You don't mind what you do.

You resurrect my dying plants,
Fill vases full of flowers,
Advised my central heating
Shouldn't be on hours and hours.

We share what happens daily,
Our joys and sorrows too,
You always encourage me
When I'm feeling blue.

I am so very grateful
For your visits every day,
This poem just says, 'Thank you,'
In a simple sort of way.

Rita Hardiman

OUR STREET

Louie cleans the windows
John repairs the cars,
Lizzie works for Oxfam
Sarah reads the stars.
Barney does the gardens
Lesley likes her drink,
Julie beats her children
Well that's what we all think,
Stanley's always fighting
The police are always there,
Lisa's always moaning
About how life ain't fair,
And I sit by the window
To see what I can see,
I wonder when they're looking back
What do they think of me?

Sally Malone

GOOD NEIGHBOURS

Nations and neighbours are yearning
For states and streets with one accord,
Purged of bitter strife, and promoting
Cities freed from falsehood and fraud.
Peace with mutual sacrifice,
Leads on to goodwill's paradise.

People are free moral agents,
Fractiousness springs from wrong choices.
Suffering caused by crass merchants,
Excite hate with bitter voices.
Malice from lawless is ruin,
Loyalty is true way to win.

Neighbour nuisance invokes the law,
Midnight music, crashing clangour,
Daubing swastikas on the door,
Stealing flowers and fruit in anger;
Devious forms of party spite,
Destroy time-honoured truth and right.

Good neighbours are just and faithful,
With helping hands for the distressed;
With games that make children cheerful,
In shadowed homes, hope is expressed.
To the joyless fresh kindness brings,
Serenity that hears bird sings,

A cup of tea holds welcome grace,
Calms weary hearts with restless pain.
Gift of flowers with smiling face,
Rallies the sad with joy again.
Pardon for trouble everywhere,
Brings blessings with an instant prayer.

James Leonard Clough

DECEIVED

Nothing was where it should be
Finding it could take a while
When suddenly a loud 'Hello'
From the owner of the smile
'I've made a pot of tea' she said
'I'll just bring you one up'
She must have known that at that time
I was desperate for a cup
'I've made you a pie' she said
'I thought you'd like a chat'
I think she was a bit put off
When she saw I had a cat
'Perhaps you'd like a sandwich?
Is there anything I can do?
If you need anything give me a shout
I'll be straight round to help you.'
She didn't like my animals
She didn't like my kids
I realised this friendship
Was headed for the skids
She didn't want to be my friend
She just wanted to poke her nose
I didn't like her anyway
That's just the way it goes.

Joy Benford

UNTITLED

A neighbour is what a neighbour should be,
Someone that lives next door to me
Not too near and not too far,
'A cup of tea?' 'Yes please, ta.'
Someone to tell your tale of woe,
When they tell theirs, it's time to go.

Julie Boitoult

REVENGE

Oh no! They're at it once again,
Making such a noise.
In my ear I've got a pain,
Think I'll send round the 'boys'.

It's four in the morning, don't they sleep?
My head it is now pounding.
I haven't slept a peep,
My posse, I'm now rounding.

Bleary eyed, and in ill humour,
I now have to go to work.
I think I'm starting with a tumour!
But my duties I mustn't shirk.

Isn't it great, all's now quiet,
I think they're all in bed.
Before I know it, I've started a riot,
I think I've lost my head.

Up at their window, they're now roaring,
To shut up all the noise.
I tell them not to be so boring,
And they're acting like little boys.

They don't like when the table's turned,
When they can't get their sleep.
But a lesson they needed to learn,
So peace and quiet we can keep.

Gail Susan Halstead

WITHOUT A SOUND

Coarse music rends the air.
For goodness sake, turn down that ghastly noise.
My head does ache. My hands are trembling
Like these flimsy cardboard walls.
My baby's sleeping.
Soon you'll hear him bawl.

You make this lonely life of mine a living hell.
If only I could crawl inside a tiny shell.
Day and night, I can't ignore this awful din.
You've no compassion or you'd see the state I'm in.

I hear your harsh roar as you strike your wife.
She's weeping loudly now.
Her life is strife yet when I speak to her
She jumps to your defence.
Her sheer devotion to you makes so little sense.

I pray each night that you will move away.
I can't go on much longer.
Day by day, I grow more nervous
And depression saps my strength.
To rid myself of you I'd go to any length.

You are the ultimate neighbour from hell!
Your kind belong inside a prison cell
For untold misery you spread around.
I wish you'd disappear without a sound.

Rosemary Thomson

NEIGHBOURS - A BREED ALONE

Neighbours - some are good, others are bad
Some . . . you wish you never had
Some are pleasant, others are not
Some you loathe - some, like a lot.

Some neighbours are *twitchers*, curtains I mean
Some keep up with the Jones' so as not to go green
Some know your business as much as you do
Some neighbours have not one face - but two!

Some neighbours will help in a crisis
Others sit back and simply don't care
There are those you can always rely on
To help. Halved trouble - trouble shared.

Some neighbours will stay for a long tome
Some others stay merely a while
Some will always make you cross or angry
A few good ones bring happiness and smiles,

There are some from whom you can borrow
There are some you know you can loan
But the one certain fact I am sure of
They stand out as a breed of their own.

Susan Merrifield

MUSICAL NEIGHBOURS

Aren't I glad that she chose the recorder,
It's a pity she cannot yet play,
I think that's *Away in a Manger,*
And really that's where it should stay,
Already we've had the dawn chorus,
And also the midnight retreat,
It's only been days since she started,
And I doubt that she'll last out the week,
It isn't that I like complaining,
It is a free country I know,
But when you teach her the recorder,
Why can't she just suck and not blow?

Michele Baston

GOOD NEIGHBOUR

I knew the day I moved in,
that friendship would be the thing.
You made me a hot cup of tea,
and said, 'Don't worry, it's free.'

Your jokes kept me going that day,
made me feel I wanted to stay.
For years now we've been good friends,
your support seems to know no end.

We still live next door to each other,
and you're like a second mother.
We watched our children grow up,
and shared both our good and bad luck.

I was right the day I moved in,
and friendship was truly the thing.
Often we share cups of tea,
and you still joke, 'Don't worry, it's free!'

Anna King

OSCAR D KOSSOLOFF

Oscar D Kossoloff, antiques and objets d'art,
Lived at the end of the high street and drove an antique car;
He had no wife nor family to lavish love upon
And was a social outcast for reasons that were wrong.
Outside of business hours Oscar took great care
To keep his car in order and free of wear and tear;
But jealous were his neighbours who angry would destroy
The pride of Oscar Kossoloff, his one and only joy.
One night with Oscar sleeping, the wicked cowards came
With petrol and some matches to set the car aflame;
He wept and suffered anguish but to the Lord he prayed
For the blessing of forgiveness, and in the village stayed.
Each time the village people passed Oscar in the street,
His head he held aloft with pride, his eyes they could not meet.
The council sat in chambers to discuss what should be done
And when they'd finished talking, the Lord knew he had won;
A few days later Oscar woke and pulled his curtains wide
To find a perfect replica of the antique car outside.
His tears he dried then ventured forth, greeted by a cheer
Of 'Oscar, please forgive us, be a friend most welcome here'
From that day on his fortune changed as he was gathered in
Amongst his neighbours' way of life, no longer full of sin;
Each day the village greeted him as rightly one of them,
And great was Oscar's happiness, thanks be to God. Amen!

E J Butler

LITTLE BRENDA BROWN

When I dwelt in the town,
Nest door to me,
Resided Mr Brown,
With his family,
Their daughter, Brenda, a sweet little girl,
At the time would be just over three, in age,
But one day at her play did herself engage,
In a puzzled mystery.

It happened one day, whilst she did play in the garden,
With her toy space, the loose earth she patted down, it to harden,
Then, slithering from below the ground, appeared an earthworm.
At the sight she shrieked a cry, then did hesitate,
Threw down her spade. Can we forgive her
For her mistake? For a worm is so like a
Sliding, gliding, snake.
Then there was heard, sound of a bird,
That flew around her head,
The bird alighted with a twitter, giving his wings
A little flitter.
Then, ere Brenda looked on,
Both worm and bird were both gone,
Leaving Brenda to meditate,
My purpose with this text,
Is to illustrate we can be here one moment, but be gone the next.

Benny H Howell

My Neighbours, My Friends

Two old people in their retirement years,
Who should be happy but are often in tears,
Their farmhouse is old and made of stone,
They live there together but yet alone.

To care for a sick mother,
Was the burden they had carried,
A sister and a brother
They never got married,
Any love for each other
Has long turned into hate,
I often do wonder,
If it was because they never found a mate.

To care for themselves now they sometimes neglect,
At times to put clean cloths on their back,
Clay tiles on the floor all covered with muck,
They look like a pair that're down on their luck.

Inside their home you'll find lots of cats,
Be careful you don't step in their wet,
An odour lingers within the air,
To bring the grey to the darkest hair.

Visitors always bring to their faces a smile,
They leave feeling they've done something worthwhile,
I know they're old and on others depend,
But me, I consider myself their friend.

Pauline Uprichard

Neighbours

My neighbours they are elderly
You may say they are old
But I think there is only me
Could be so very bold.

They listen very closely when I have a moan
Sitting there in silence without even a groan
We try to win the lottery and say what we will do
But when it comes to Saturday
We always end with two.

Ken looks all around then he says with glee
'If I won it all I'd buy a black Bentley.'
Emily says 'You have both got stars in your eyes'
But Emily is the only one who is so very wise.

When I lost my mother, around Emily came
Even though my neighbour is very, very lame.
'Come round to our house, don't sit there and grieve
You can come and sit here whilst awaiting Steve.'
With neighbours like ours, what else can be desired
Hope we are quite like them
When we are both retired.

M S Richmond

NEIGHBOUR FROM HELL

Here is a story I must tell
Of a neighbour straight from hell.
I was only just a seven year old boy
My three-wheeled bike, my pride and joy.
Next door there lived Winnie Moss
My mum showed her who was boss.
For her window she would stare
She come out with her mum's wheelchair.
Up and down the road I rode in clover
Till she tried to push me over.
I called her the old witch
To my mum I'd go and snitched.
Was she mad or just plain sick,
Did she have an old broomstick?
I can remember her still
Me just still, very ill.
I still recall that name
As home from hospital I came
To her it must have been fun
But why pick on a child so *young*?

Colin Allsop

FROM HEAVEN TO HELL OVERNIGHT

Marrying a second time I moved to a fresh home,
Believing how I'd lived before was way I'd carry on,
People living round me were much the same as me,
Making friends should not be hard, I would live happily,
Then family from in a house, which backed on to ours,
Changed character right overnight, we found we were at war,
On garden we took pride in, they rubbish threw each day,
Stand staring through our windows when supposedly at play.
Yell our names continually, ride cycles up our path,
Put fish-hooks in my washing. - That gave them a big laugh!
Language their mother used, before I'd never heard,
Not even Irish navvies would use such dreadful words.
When we would rest, they'd bang and shout, would not go away,
Their garden was like a rubbish tip, more added every day.
Father's constant hammering would ruin each weekend.
I went to try and reason, but fell and arm did bend.
It was badly broken, I was bruised from head toe,
There was no choice at all for me; to hospital must go.
Council now have given us peace just for a short spell,
Legal measures they enforced to curb neighbours from hell.

Barbara Goode

THE NEW NEIGHBOURS

I suppose the new people over the back are neighbours
But they didn't move here to our leafy lane
In deepest Surrey to settle.
This is a real village with a green and river
A village pub and stores. The old boy was a bricklayer
And lived here for fifty years or more.
But the new people, our neighbours
Have come here to speculate.

For months they just cut the grass
The wife sits on a mower with baby on her knee
And mows the field keeping it neat, this was a field
Of dandelion and burdock where sheep used to graze.
On Sundays the place fills up with cars as young families
Come to play cricket.
Jolly nice chaps, Henry, Timothy and Wills
But its not cricket to speculate.

Now plans are with Planning, the surveyors have taken lines
Of sight readings with theodolites
Grass verges and hedges would disappear
Men have measured the girths of trees
Sycamores would have to go.
We look down the garden through silver birch and hazels
See patches of sky and a line of mature oaks and beech.
Instead there would be executive houses called Thistlewood
Or Sheephatch Close.
And in this sylvan setting, agents would flock to sell it.

Our neighbours would move on up market
They are just passing through our village
Hoping to speculate.

Jan Ingram McCaffery

LOOK THROUGH MY EYES

Take a good look
at that monster they call Cook.
With the sound like a child cries,
can't you hear the calls for him to be crucified?

Is the victim's blood right?
Now look at him with my sight.
Consider now *my* pain
should I have to damn him, never to return again!

Hard lesson, isn't it!
That I do judge as I see fit.
And should, before he die, call to me 'Forgive,'
I would! I died that he might live.

Hate his crime, but pray for him;
For in my sight is your hidden sin.
Have I not given you my father's wealth?
So love your neighbour as yourself.

Philip Trivett

Untitled

I'm a mother of three
so I'm going to write you see
as I have an enemy next door.
If we happen to meet in the street
she'll hit me to the floor.
Myself I would rather run a mile or two
than stand my ground,
because that's something I dare not do.
That evil woman, you know she has no grace,
to stand and punch my baby in the face.
Bruises galore from the woman next door.
Now sad my heart, I cannot smile
fear within me I run that mile.
The neighbour she scares me in the night
fear never eases through morning light.
I cannot face another day, I'm tired, sad and done,
I've lost all hope, now life is just no fun.
Fears I've got an awful lot, I've worries by the score
I'm just about fed up with the neighbour forcing my door.
The police, they don't care, which really is unfair
she spits in my face, the police state they have no case.
Bruises all over, what a mess,
so, consequently I had to go
and move to a different address.
Now I feel much safer, it would be really fine
if you'd take a not of the following
just in case you want to drop me a line.

Janet Smith

THE FOLK NEXT DOOR

To love your neighbour as yourself
Is often hard to do,
Well-meaning as they mean to be,
Sometimes pastures new
Seem to be the only way
To rid yourself of those
Who intrude more than they ought
And in your business nose:
'It's only me - I'll not stay long'
Yet all the time you know
Another quiet evening's gone,
Whenever will they go?
Still good friends are hard to find
And there's no guarantee,
We could take the plunge and move
Where neighbours might well be
The sort who really come from hell,
Just think of you or me
Living next door to some of those
They portray on TV.
So our blessings we'll just count,
The folk who live next door
Have been our friends for many a year,
Who could ask for more?

Peter Fordham

Frankly

I have feelings of ambivalence,
Every time I glance across the road,
For in the house opposite mine,
Lives a dog, a boy, a snake and a toad.

The dog knows nothing, he is simply hairy,
He terrorises children, for his bark is scary,
The snake slithers out to admonish and scold,
I catch its beady eye, and my blood runs cold.

The toad croaks, his eyes pop, he is an ugly creature,
His body wobbles wetly - not an attractive feature.
Toad has to jump at snake's command, he is simply not a winner,
Oh! If only snake would gobble him up and eat him for her dinner.

The boy, such a small boy, now one could care for him,
He has a round honest face, and a cheeky little grin,
It is a great pity that he lives in the house across the road,
With a mother who's a snake and a father who's a toad.

Pauline Nash

THE NEIGHBOURS

Each morning very early, upon the stroke of six,
The Smiths are cleaning windows, that's how they get their fix.
For cleaning is their passion, shared by both you see
Better than a whisky tot, or a cup of *Rosie Lee*.

Wiping every window ledge, the second floor as well
They polish up the dustbin lid, the gate and front door bell
This obsessive ritual is every day complete
Before I've had my breakfast, and Postie's on the street.

In their regimented garden, grass may not grow askew.
For if it did then, God forbid! The air would soon turn blue.
A weed dare not rear its ugly head amid the beds so neat
For always 'at the ready,' is a spray for its defeat.

No offspring now remains at home, no-one to make a mess
So why the constant cleaning? Is anybody's guess.
The house and gardens I suspect, fulfil their every need
To occupy their golden years, or they too would go to seed.

Hazel Vambria Walters

GOOD SAMARITAN

Who's my guardian angel?
Who's my special friend?
Who brings shopping when I'm sick
And library books to lend?
Who daily checks my curtains,
Looking for a sign
That I'm about my daily chores,
Or shares a glass of wine?

Who plants flowers by my door?
Who keeps a second key
When I'm at home, alone all day,
With no-one else to see?
Who's my *Good Samaritan*
Without whom I'd be lost?
It is my caring neighbour
Who *never* counts the cost.

Pauline Pullan

BLOOD AND WATER
(Neighbours of the Red Indian)

They had given their all, now one last stand.
With men at the ready, he watched and waited
For the signal to remove the snake from his land.
The foreign intruder, despised and hated.

. . . and every move was carefully planned.

His dark, deep brown eyes were fierce and set.
No sound could be heard, save the sun-warmed wind.
To the brave men who died, he owed much debt.
A fight to the death, he vowed in his mind.

. . . and promises made were promises kept.

The truce and peace talks had come to an end.
His terms for peace were refused or ignored.
Exposed were the lice who professed to be friend
Conniving and insults to be no more endured.

. . . and men will die round the river bend.

The signal is made and the moment has come.
Defiant he raises his arm, straight and high.
Each man prepared for what has to be done,
As plumes of white smoke lifted to the sky.

. . . and the river turned red when the battle was won.

David Barrow

NEIGHBOURS

I'm sure the world as we perceive
Is exactly what they want us to b'lieve.
Life on Mars - Why do we doubt?
Who says its an echo we hear when we shout?
Perhaps it's a neighbour from a different moon
Who landed on earth ten light years too soon.

I'm sure the world that we all see
Is far from alien and martian free.
After all, why should it be?
Who says ours is the only galaxy?
There are probably others the same as ours,
With rulers who possess stronger powers.

I'm sure the world that's surrounding me
Is still a total mystery.
People see aliens every day -
Who are we to dispute what they say?

Chrissi

OUR POSTMAN

No it's not Postman Pat
I think it's brother Bill
But life gets very strenuous
When he has to climb that hill

From Daventry to Welton
He comes out every day
And he brings our mail around
In his usual cheery way

When the weather is nasty
He has to wear his mac
He is always very glad
When he's finished and gets back

He's such a caring chap
To people when they're ill
We all think the world of him
That's our postman, Bill

D Sheasby

BLESS MY NEIGHBOUR

As I sat here, in the home, the other day,
I though about my old life far away;
I was looking at the road show, the one about antiques,
When on the telly was my old friend, Mrs Meeks.

She was my next door neighbour, in the world I've left behind,
She'd visit me, and shop for me, she really was most kind.
When I grew too frail to live alone, they sent me to this place;
I said 'Goodbye' to Mrs Meeks, while tears ran down my face.

She asked me for a keepsake, as she eyed the kitchen clock,
Older than me, still keeping time, with its gentle tick and tock.
And here she was, in front of me, the old clock in her hand.
The expert looked at it and said, 'My word, my dear, that's grand;

Would you like to know how much it's worth? Ten thousand pounds
 at least!
That money could have all been mine, oh, what a lovely feast.
Of things I could have bought with it; but my old neighbour's got it,
And all that lovely lolly will be going in her pocket.

I'd better say 'Good luck' to her, but wonder if she knew,
When she asked for it, that the clock was worth a bob or two.

Michael Darwood

DIFFERENT TO US

Our neighbours are very different to us,
Are quick to offer lifts, when we miss the bus.
They keep animals and have a garden shed,
Help us with shopping if anyone's ill in bed.
We don't go round for cups of coffee or tea,
Their dogs bark loudly, for quiet we do not plea.
Know in a crisis our neighbours we would call,
Because they do live right next door after all!

Susan Mullinger

THE STATE AND ME

And can I really reach out
from my life's cramped confines
into the hard yoke of race
or the aims and cold claims
of just one nation-state
for the rest of my life?

If there is no peace
can I alone
end strife?
If food is scarce can I
increase supplies
and give to those who lack?
Whatever can I do
to save fellow citizens
from those who govern by the use
of concealing secrecy rules
and unjust laws?

I know nature set me
within a race and state
but she gave limited vision to my eyes!
I cannot comprehend
or see where I fit
in a great
independent nation
whose future rests on me
and the way I act from now on!

Dan Pugh

OUR NEIGHBOURS FROM HEAVEN

Our neighbours from
Heaven
Live next door to
Us
And do not
Cause a
Fuss
Because when we go
Away
They look after
Our house
Every day
Janet and
Harry
Are their
Names
And we hope one
Day
We can do the
Same
Now and
Again

Coleen Bradshaw

IN THE VAST EXPANSE

Are we alone in the universe,
As a solitary inhabited planet,
Earth's creations in the vast expanse of it all?

Are we unique,
Or out there on neighbouring planets,
Do we coexist with other forms of life?

In a world once thought to be flat,
Science made the breakthrough,
Proving otherwise,

One day will it be proved,
That there are living species on other worlds,
Maybe not of the same appearance as ourselves?

We read through the media,
Of alien encounters in many guises,
The convinced are classed as gullible,

The non believers as having a closed mind,
Whatever our own beliefs,
It is a question that we cannot dismiss lightly,

God was at the beginning of all creation,
Not just of this earth and the universe known to exist,
But of the beyond, the inaccessible, the unknown,

In His great wisdom it would seem,
That He would fill some of the created mass with life,
That can think and operate intelligently,

What was the point of its creation otherwise?
It would seem fruitless if not for this reason,
To have an expansion of space undiscovered,

If extraterrestrial neighbours are out there,
Then to believe in God they are of his conception,
In the many mansions of heaven we may be privileged to know.

Ann G Wallace

THE NEIGHBOUR FROM HELL!

A little sheltered complex,
Hidden out of sight.
Where elderly and disabled,
Could rest peacefully at night.
Doctors had said the residents,
All were in need of care.
So pull a cord in an emergency,
And a warden would be there.

So this little complex,
On the outskirts of the city.
Donated to the residents,
By the Council out of pity.
A place of peace and tranquillity,
Where one might end one's days.
A haven blessed by God,
In oh so many ways.

No-one saw the danger,
No-one could foretell,
That the peace would soon be shattered,
When a neighbour came from hell.
In a drunken stupor,
He'd stagger on his way.
Bringing hordes of drunken friends,
By night and then by day.

Children who came to visit him,
Allowed to bang on windows and doors.
And an alsatian fouled the area,
Till I could stand no more.
But the Council wasn't interested,
Their duty to the residents done.
So what if our new neighbour,
Wanted a little fun?

So now my temper's rising,
I'll not give up the fight.
To get someone to listen,
And put our complex right.
Then we may sleep again,
Knowing all is well.
And for our drunken neighbour?
Send him back to hell.

M Muirhead

NEIGHBOURS FROM MARS

Now that a probe from Earth has landed,
The red planet beckons
In all its arid, scarlet splendour.

I see a strange face on the TV news,
Formed from the barren red rock
Of the neighbouring planet we know as Mars.

Was it the image of a man buried there, in pomp and ceremony,
A leader like the pharaohs of Egypt,
The last survivor of a forgotten age?

Heavy and simple are his features,
Like an idol in a Peruvian temple.
Maybe his people built their civilisation.

Perhaps Earth ships will land there one day,
Fly a flag with our own blue planet on it.
Not a war of the worlds, but a meeting of minds.

David Tallach

NUMBER TEN

From cussing and cursing, inclusive of swear,
A language so ancient, it gets them nowhere.
To ranting and raving at the edge of the path,
Immaturely committed, as the child in the class.
Feeling highly intelligent, the best and the all,
As the kid in the school yard, when kicking the ball,
To hurl to the rooftop, with expressions of glee;
Now a forty plus bully, adjoins our property.

Sara Russell, Golden Eagles MCC

THE NEIGHBOUR FROM HELL

I though I knew the chap next door well
But I was mistaken, he's the neighbour from hell
He cuts my bush down without asking my permission
And if you say anything, he won't even listen

He parks his car across my drive so I can't get out
He really is impossible without a doubt
He plays loud music all day and all night
He won't turn it down, he thinks it's his right

He just bad mouths you and swears abuse
To reason with the man is no use
He makes snide comments to residents in the road
I wish I could afford to change my abode

We can all hear him bellowing when gets home
Either at his wife or to someone down the phone
It is not just myself but many have felt his wrath
He upsets almost everyone that he comes across

He rows all the time with his poor wife
He must give her a terrible life
At the least little thing he'll scream and shout
He really is a loud-mouthed lout

They never have friends or family come to stay
They know what he is like, they keep away
But they say you get your just deserts in the end
He will probably end up alone without kin or friend.

Linda Brown

MARITAL BLISS

Neighbours are best
when they're seen and not heard
but we have been blessed
with a *right* noisy herd
(of elephants, you'd think
as they move 'round the house)
whereas *we* always slink about
quiet as a mouse!
The arguments we hear through the living room wall
are far worse than ours are -
in fact not at *all* gentle and civilised as *we* try to be
when we're airing our grievances *(usually)*.
I think I will write them a letter and say:
'Will you please keep the noise down or else move away.'
It's funny in all the time we've been together
that no-one's complained - no really, not ever -
about all the noise from our frequent 'domestics,'
... but when you throw mud
you do find that less sticks
to yourself and your spouse
(if the truth's to be told)
when the folk in your *own* house
are all good as gold.

Yvonne Sewell

IN-LAWS

Caring and sharing with folk that you know
Can be a difficult thing to do
To learn to indulge your personal need
This can only be handled by a few;
My two special neighbours remind me of that
As it is in-laws through the bricks next door
When I was depressed they rallied around
To become part of my husband's unique core.
Through their kindliness to him
They gave birth and life to me
Allowing me to find my feet
With just slight control of life's key
And despite all the black that came from me
They've stayed trusting and caring all around
Marching through those dark and dismal days
Making me no longer lost, but found.

Carol Dunn

ON A HOT DUSTY STREET

I met her on a hot dusty street,
in her arms a colourful bouquet
of freshly-cut garden flowers.
'They're for my mother,' she said.
'She's dead eight years today.'

I didn't know her mother,
and I only know her as the neighbour
who makes treats and meals
and small happy occasions
for the chronic patients
in our psychiatric hospital.

Goodness has a feeling
a flavour, a colour
like those fresh flowers
to a mother's memory,
laid across a soft arm
on a hot dusty street.

Teresita Durkan

LIFE AT 80

Songs of Praise News at Ten
Stare and doze
The life I chose
Ghosts are my neighbours now

Busy, idle, idly busy
Never wanting really
Never knowing much
Wanting vaguely, never knowing
Who dreams but me?
Because ghosts are my neighbours now

I think I wait
I know I wonder
I think I know
I know not what

Wide eyed and weary
I watch
Waiting and bleary
I watch
Thinking I know

News at Ten and Songs of Praise
Out of focus
Put the sound up colour haze

Scared and hopeful
I look at the screen

At the ghosts of my neighbours

Switch the sound down see the action
Will they surface
Waiting knowing?

Veda Dovaston

NEIGHBOURS

There was a time when this word
Had one meaning, how absurd,
It meant people who lived next door
They could be either rich or poor.

The days of peace are long since past
TV programmes are here to last
It is said by popular choice
I wonder how many did give voice

Do not count me with this throng
I don't know the soap's theme song
I've better things to do than sit
In front of a box even though I knit

So neighbours still mean this to me
The man who has cut down my tree
Who sprayed along the boundary fence
And won't give me my recompense

Who now will not communicate
And throws his weeds over my gate
Lets his dog water my flowers
Plus plays loud music for hours and hours

There's not much to choose between
The man next door and the TV screen
But still I try to neighbourly be
And trust my neighbour will reason see.

Sylvia Chandler

HEALTHY LIVING NEIGHBOURS
(From the Good Life)

'Wrap your knee with a cabbage leaf,
It will give you great relief.'
'A cork in bed will save you from cramp.'
'To brighten up your golden locks,
Dried camomile flowers,' and then for shocks
'Breathe deeply and then repeat
A prayer or mantra with some meadowsweet.'

'I hope these tips are helping you
As I'd like to suggest a nettle brew,'
'Dandelion leaves and the wayside yarrow
Are there for us all to load in a barrow.'

'No doctors' fees you need to spend,
Just treat your garden as a friend
And fields and woods in the great outdoor
Will bring you happiness galore!
You'll find they are not so far away,
And the best neighbours you'll have to stay.
Live long and happy with Mother Earth -
You'll find you've discovered a rebirth!'

'Those little seeds you plant today
Will shed joyful living along your way.
The trees, the plants and all the grasses,
God has provided for the masses.
They are all living next door to you,
Waiting ready for what *you* can do.'

You may think health nuts are all cranks
And do not wish to copy their pranks!
But I guess they've got the right idea,
And some good advice from them we hear.

Beatrice Wilson

INFORMATION

We hope you have enjoyed reading this book - and that you will continue to enjoy it in the coming years.

If you like reading and writing poetry drop us a line, or give us a call, and we'll send you a free information pack.

Write to :-
**Triumph House Information
1-2 Wainman Road
Woodston
Peterborough
PE2 7BU
(01733) 230749**